KINGFISHER
An imprint of Larousse plc
Elsley House, 24–30 Great Titchfield Street,
London, W1P 7AD

First published by Kingfisher 1994
2 4 6 8 10 9 7 5 3 1

Copyright © Larousse plc 1994
Text © Michael Benton 1994
Illustrations © Ann Winterbotham 1990

All rights reserved.
A CIP catalogue record for this book
is available from the British Library.

ISBN 1 85697 239 9

Series editor: Sue Nicholson
Editors: Brigid Avison, Hazel Poole
Cover design: Terry Woodley
Design: Ben White Associates
Cover illustrations: Ann Winterbotham
Ann Winterbotham's illustrations previously published
in *All About Dinosaurs* Kingfisher 1990
Illustrations on pp 13 & 23 by Maggie Brand
(Maggie Mundy Agency)
Typeset by SPAN, Lingfield, Surrey
Printed in Great Britain by BPC Paulton Books Limited

LITTLE LIBRARY

Discovering Dinosaurs

Michael Benton

Illustrated by Ann Winterbotham

Contents

What were dinosaurs?	7
How big were they?	8
The giants	10
Dinosaur dinners	12
Meat-eaters	14
Plant-eaters	16
Nests and eggs	18
Living in groups	20
Defence	22
A big puzzle	24
Museum monsters	26
Saying the names	28
Index	29

What were dinosaurs?

Dinosaurs lived on Earth millions of years ago. They belonged to a group of animals called reptiles. Dinosaur means 'terrible reptile'. Today's reptiles include snakes, crocodiles and lizards. There are no dinosaurs alive today.

Some dinosaurs were big and fierce...

...and others were small and fast.

How big were they?

Dinosaurs came in all shapes and sizes. Some were as big as an elephant. Others were the size of a small chicken. Apatosaurus would have been tall enough to look through the second floor window of a house!

Do you know the names of all these dinosaurs?

① ②

ANSWERS

1 Struthiomimus
2 Stegosaurus
3 Apatosaurus
4 Iguanodon
5 Triceratops
6 Compsognathus

Turn to page 28 to find out how to say these names.

The giants

Until recently, scientists believed that Brachiosaurus was the largest dinosaur that lived. But now huge dinosaur bones have been dug up which belonged to some even bigger animals. These dinosaurs all looked like Brachiosaurus and have been named Supersaurus, Ultrasaurus and Seismosaurus.

At 20 metres long, Brachiosaurus (1) was really quite small if you compare its size with recent dinosaur finds. Supersaurus (2) was 28 metres long and Seismosaurus (3) was massive, at around 45 metres long.

Dinosaur dinners

Some dinosaurs, like Stegosaurus, were vegetarians – they ate only plants. Others, such as Allosaurus, were meat-eaters.

Allosaurus tried to eat Stegosaurus.

DINO SANDWICHES

Here's how YOU can have dinosaurs for dinner!

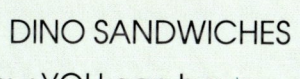

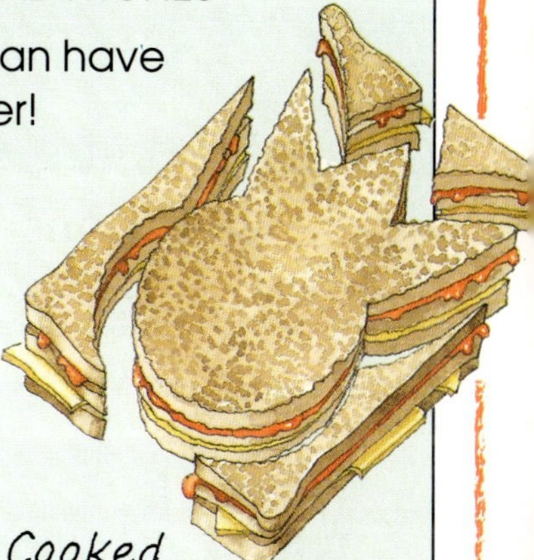

1 Make several rounds of different sandwiches filled with your favourite spread. Then cut them into dinosaur footprints.

Cooked meat

Cheese

2 Cut out cold meats or cheese slices into simple dinosaur shapes. Decorate them with peanuts or with scraps of cucumber and other vegetables.

Here are a couple of ideas to start with. See if your friends can guess the names of the different dinosaurs.

Meat-eaters

Tyrannosaurus was the most terrifying of the meat-eaters. It stood 6 metres high and could run very fast at times. It had a huge mouth with very sharp teeth.

Tyrannosaurus trod on its lunch, tearing off great mouthfuls with its teeth.

Plant-eaters

Iguanodon was a big and gentle plant-eater. It was 10 metres long and had blunt, broad teeth for grinding up tough leaves. It also had a very sharp thumb claw!

Iguanodon used its long tongue to pull leaves into its mouth.

A NASTY BITE

Some of the small plant-eaters had very sharp teeth called fangs. They may have used their fangs to snap at the meat-eaters who attacked and tried to eat them for lunch.

Nests and eggs

Dinosaurs laid their eggs in nests, just as birds and reptiles do today. Maiasaura was a caring parent. The name 'Maiasaura' means 'good mother reptile'.

The mother dug a big round hollow in the sand and laid 20 or 30 eggs.
▽

△
Then she covered the nest with leaves to keep the eggs warm.

OUT OF THE EGG

Maiasaura's eggs took about one month to hatch. By then, each baby was already about 40 or 50 centimetres long.

Maiasaura looked after her babies and fed them with leaves.

Living in groups

Triceratops had three sharp horns on its head. It lived in large family groups, and moved about just as elephants do today, grazing on tree leaves and other plants.

If Tyrannosaurus tried to attack a group of Triceratops, they formed a circle around their babies to keep them safe. They then swung their great horns to fight off their attacker.

Triceratops means 'three-horned face'.

Defence

Stegosaurus's weapons were the sharp spikes on the end of its tail. The bony plates along its back may also have stopped meat-eaters from trying to eat it.

MAKE A MOSAIC STEGOSAURUS

A mosaic is a picture made from tiny pieces of coloured stones or paper.

1 Draw the shape of a Stegosaurus on to a large sheet of thin card.

2 Tear out lots of pieces of coloured paper, all about 3 centimetres square, from some old magazines.

3 Stick the pieces down, slightly overlapping, so there are no gaps.

4 Trim around the shape to neaten the edges. Then colour in a face.

A big puzzle

About 65 million years ago, the dinosaurs died out. No one knows exactly why this happened. A giant rock from outer space might have crashed into the Earth, sending great clouds of dust into the air and changing the weather.

Plants would have died and then the dinosaurs may have died of hunger.

Fossils are the stony remains of animals and plants that died long ago. It can take years to dig out a whole skeleton.

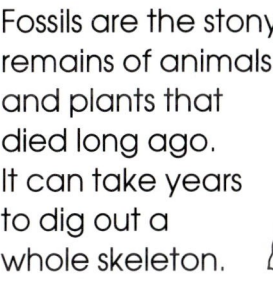

Today, scientists can find out about dinosaurs by studying stony fossils of their bones which have been found all around the world.

The bones are carefully cleaned...

...and then joined up to make skeletons.

25

Museum monsters

There are lots of museums where you can see complete skeletons. Some also have models showing what living dinosaurs may have looked like.

Saying the names

Allosaurus (AL-oh-SAW-rus)

Apatosaurus (a-PAT-oh-SAW-rus)

Brachiosaurus (BRAK-ee-oh-SAW-rus)

Compsognathus (komp-SOG-na-thus)

Iguanodon (Ig-WA-noh-don)

Maiasaura (MY-a-SAW-ra)

Seismosaurus (SIZE-mo-SAW-rus)

Stegosaurus (STEG-oh-SAW-rus)

Struthiomimus (STROOTH-ee-oh-MY-mus)

Supersaurus (super-SAW-rus)

Triceratops (try-SER-a-tops)

Tyrannosaurus (tie-RAN-oh-SAW-rus)

Ultrasaurus (ultra-SAW-rus)

Index

Allosaurus   12
Apatosaurus   8–9
bones   25, 26–7
Brachiosaurus   10
Compsognathus   9
eggs   18–19
fossil   25
Iguanodon   9, 16–17
Maiasaura   18–19
Seismosaurus   10
Stegosaurus   8, 12, 22–3
Struthiomimus   8
Supersaurus   10
teeth   14–15, 16–17
Triceratops   9, 20–21
Tyrannosaurus   14–15
Ultrasaurus   10